Step-by-Step

Papier Mâché

Judy Balchin

Heinemann Library

Published by Heinemann Library,
an imprint of Reed Educational & Professional Publishing,
100 N. LaSalle, Suite 1010
Chicago, IL 60602
Customer Service 888-454-2279
Visit our website at www.heinemannlibrary.com

Photographs and design copyright © Search Press Limited 2000
Text copyright © Judy Balchin 2000
Originated by Graphics '91, Singapore
Designed by Search Press
Printed in Italy by L.E.G.O.

05 04 03 02 01
10 9 8 7 6 5 4 3 2 1

Library of Congress Cataloging-in-Publication Data
Balchin, Judy.
    Papier mâché / Judy Balchin.
        p. cm. -- (Step-by-step)
    Includes bibliographical references and index.
    ISBN 1-57572-328-X
    1. Papier-mâchâ--Juvenile literature. [1. Papier-mâchâ. 2. Handicraft.] I. Title: Papier mâché. II. Title. III. Step-by-step (Heinemann Library)

TT871 .B35 2000
745.54'2--dc21

00-038889

Acknowledgments
The author and publishers are grateful to the following for permission to reproduce copyright material:
Christie's Images, p.5.

Photographs: Search Press Studios

Every effort has been made to contact copyright holders of any material reproduced in this book. Any omissions will be rectified in subsequent printings if notice is given to the publisher.

To my husband John. Here's to the next twenty-five years!

Some words are shown in bold, **like this**. You can find out what they mean by looking in the glossary.

When this sign is used in the book, it means that adult supervision is needed.

REMEMBER!
Ask an adult to help you when you see this sign.

Contents

Introduction

Papier mâché is a French term that means "chewed or mashed paper." It was invented in China in the first part of the second century. The Chinese discovered that it was possible to make many items out of papier mâché. They created pots and even helmets that they covered with varnish to make them hard-wearing and durable. Over time, mankind became more and more ambitious, and by the seventeenth century even a church was being built using papier mâché! In the following century, a man named Charles Ducrest drew up plans for making tables, bookcases, and even houses, boats, and bridges using either papier mâché alone, or wood or iron structures covered in papier mâché.

Although you will not be making churches, houses, or boats in this book, you will be able to have lots of fun with papier mâché—from making a simple photograph frame to modeling a cat. I have taken the inspiration for the items from past civilizations. You will go on a journey to discover Celtic and Indian decoration, Mexican and Gothic design, Egyptian, Aztec, Roman, and African art.

There are two main ways of making papier mâché: layering and pulping. You will be using both methods in the projects in this book, sometimes combining both on one piece. Each project shows you a different way of using papier mâché and suggests how you can decorate your pieces.

If you are interested in recycling, then this book is definitely for you. Old newspapers, cardboard tubing, and candy wrappers are just a few of the things that you will be working with, so start saving! Before you throw anything away, ask yourself if it could be used in a papier mâché project. An old plastic bottle or cardboard box can spark off an amazing idea, so keep your eyes open. In particular, watch for colored papers, beads, feathers, string, and foil papers—anything that could be used to decorate your creations.

We all like to make things, but to make something totally unique has a special meaning. As you become more confident using papier mâché, I am sure you will come up with lots of your own ideas and designs. Be bold, experiment, but most of all, have lots of fun.

Opposite Many people think that papier mâché is used only by children to make simple and inexpensive items like masks. However, this richly decorated box, called a casket, was made from papier mâché in the 1770s. It must have been bought by a very wealthy or important person, because it would have cost a great deal of money to decorate it so beautifully.

Materials

The best thing about papier mâché is that it is such an inexpensive hobby. You will not need all the things listed on this page to begin. Many of the materials that you need to get started can be found in your own home. Keep a box handy so that you can store old newspapers, tissue and colored paper, cardboard boxes and tubes. All these will come in handy for papier mâché projects.

Gesso is used to prime a surface before decorating with *colored paint*. The colored paint used in this book is *acrylic*. This paint covers well and is hard-wearing. *Poster paint* can also be used, but this needs to be protected with a coat of *varnish*. Varnish can also be used to give a shiny appearance. It is best to use paint from a **palette** rather than straight from the pot.

Sheets of *newspaper* can be used to cover your work surface. Strips of newspaper are used for the basic layering technique. *Paper pulp* is used for modeling or applying to a surface for a textured look. You can buy it in packs at craft stores or make your own from pieces of newspaper.

Paint can be applied with a *paintbrush*. An assortment of sizes are used in this book. The end of a paintbrush can be used to make holes in the pulp. A piece of *sponge* can also be used to apply paint. A *toothbrush* is used for spattering paint and a *potato* is used to stamp paint onto a surface.

You will need a selection of *bowls*, a *colander* or *strainer*, *wooden spoon*, *tablespoon*, and *mug* for making pulp and mixing up wallpaper paste. A *cooling rack* is ideal for drying pieces on. *Plastic wrap* is used to seal bowls containing already mixed wallpaper paste. It can also be used to line a mold before it is covered with paper pulp.

Non-toxic *wallpaper paste* is used for all papier mâché work. *Multipurpose glue* is added to wallpaper paste to strengthen the mix. It can also be used as a glue. If you **dilute** multipurpose glue with water to the consistency of thin cream, it can be used as a varnish. It should be applied with a *paste brush*. Always wash your hands after handling glue and wallpaper paste.

Scissors are used to cut paper, posterboard and string. A *craft knife* is used to cut thick cardboard. Always ask an adult to do this for you as craft knives are very sharp. Craft knives should be used on a *cutting board*. A *vegetable knife* is used to cut a shape in a potato so that you can print with it.

Poster or *paper board* (for example, from a cereal box) is ideal as a base for many papier mâché projects. *Cardboard* is also used. This comes in two thicknesses: double **corrugated** and single corrugated. Cardboard boxes are fine. *Cardboard tubing* comes in different widths, and this is also used.

A *ruler* and *pencil* are used for measuring pieces of cardboard and drawing straight lines. A pencil is also used to trace around patterns.

Masking tape is used to hold pieces of posterboard in position before applying pasted newspaper strips. It is also used for masking off areas from paint.

Beads, feathers, ribbon, and string are all used for decoration. Beads can be threaded on *leather thong*. *Colored foil paper* can be glued to a surface for a sparkly look or scrunched into balls and used as jewel-like decorations. Old candy wrappers are ideal.

Techniques

Papier mâché is not a difficult craft, but it is worth reading through this techniques section carefully before you begin the projects.

Note Papier mâché is messy, so it is best to cover your workspace with a large piece of newspaper. Alternatively, use a plastic cloth that can be wiped down and used again.

Transferring a design to cardboard

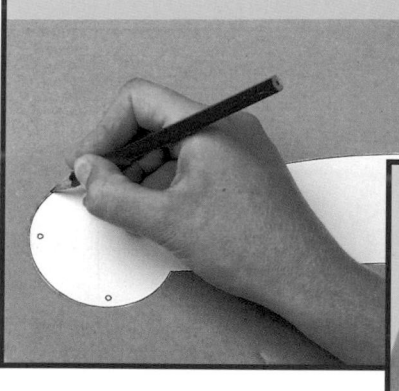

Patterns are provided on pages 30–31. These can be enlarged on a photocopier. Cut around the photocopied pattern, then lay it on posterboard or single **corrugated** cardboard and trace around the edge with a pencil. Cut around the line with scissors.

> (!) Double corrugated cardboard is much tougher than single, and it needs to be cut with a craft knife. Ask an adult to do this for you—craft knives are very sharp.

Preventing warping

Sometimes papier mâché pieces made from a cardboard base can **warp** during the drying process. To prevent this, always give your base cardboard shape a coat of slightly **diluted** multipurpose glue.

Paste both sides of the cardboard. Let it dry naturally on a cooling rack, turning it occasionally so that it dries evenly. When completely dry, the cardboard can be layered with newspaper strips.

Note When multipurpose glue is dry, it can be difficult to remove. Wear an apron or old shirt to protect your clothes.

Mixing up the paste

Pour one pint (half a liter) of water into a bowl and sprinkle with wallpaper paste. The instructions on the packet will tell you how much to use. Stir the mixture well and leave it for fifteen minutes. Then add a tablespoon of multipurpose glue to strengthen the paste.

Note Once wallpaper paste has been made up, it can be stored in a bowl fitted with an airtight lid or sealed with plastic wrap. It will last for several days if kept in the refrigerator.

Layering with newspaper strips

Layering involves pasting strips of newspaper with a mixture of wallpaper paste and multipurpose glue, and then pressing them onto a base. When dry, the pieces will be strong but light, and ready for decorating.

Tear small strips of newspaper for small structures and larger strips for bigger items. Use your fingers to smear paste onto the strips of paper, then press them onto your base so that they overlap each other. Smooth the strips down as you work.

Note Complete one layer at a time. You will be told how many layers to apply for each project. To help you keep count of the number of layers you have worked, you can apply one layer of colored newspaper, followed by one layer of black and white and so on.

Using paper pulp

Papier mâché pulp can be bought from craft stores. It is a powdered paper that is mixed with water to create a modeling material. You can also make your own, as shown here. Once you have mixed the pulp, it can be stored in a plastic bag in the refrigerator until needed.

1 Tear enough small pieces of newspaper to fill a mug when packed tightly.

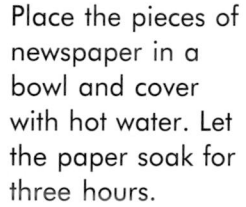

2 Place the pieces of newspaper in a bowl and cover with hot water. Let the paper soak for three hours.

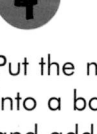

3 Transfer the soaked paper into a colander or strainer. Squeeze the pieces together so that the water runs out and the paper forms a mash.

4 Put the mash into a bowl and add a tablespoon of multipurpose glue and a tablespoon of wallpaper paste mixture.

5 Mix everything together with your fingers.

Note When you have completed a pulped papier mâché project, let it dry naturally. The pulp shrinks as it dries and sometimes creates small splits or cracks in the surface. These can be disguised by smearing a little more paper pulp into them and allowing the project to dry again.

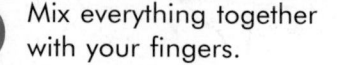

Priming and painting

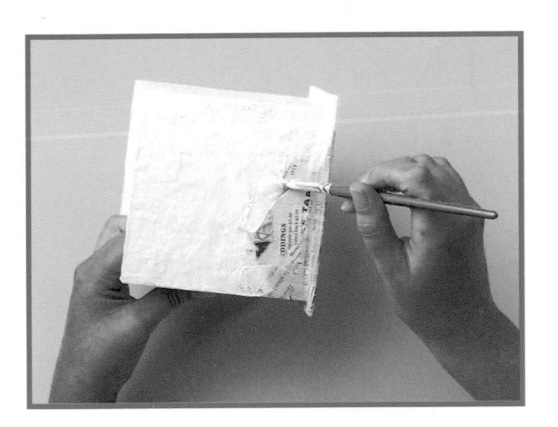

Priming means preparing a surface so that it can be decorated with colored paint. Use **gesso** to do this. You may need two coats to cover the newspaper print completely. Allow the first coat to dry before applying the second.

The projects in this book are decorated with acrylic paint because it covers well, is hard-wearing, and does not need to be varnished. Once the white primer is dry, paint your finished object in colors of your choice.

Note All items painted with poster paint should be protected with a coat of varnish. You can use **diluted** multipurpose glue for this. If you do use poster paint, mix it with a little multipurpose glue before you apply it. This will prevent the paint from smearing when you varnish it.

Celtic Goblet

Celtic craftsmen were well-known for their metal work. The **goblet** in this project is made to look like metal, but it is actually made out of an old plastic drink bottle. The surface is covered with pulp to create a textured surface that looks like beaten metal. It is decorated with metallic paint and glass beads to create a container that is truly fit for a king! Remember that this goblet is purely decorative and cannot be used to drink out of.

YOU WILL NEED
Plastic drink bottle
Single corrugated cardboard
Paper pulp • Glass beads
Metallic acrylic paint • Paintbrush
Palette • Multipurpose glue
Scissors • Masking tape
Newspaper

1 Cut off the top third of a plastic drink bottle.

2 Cut a circle of single **corrugated** cardboard approximately 2½ inches (6.5 cm) in diameter. Use masking tape to attach the cardboard circle to the top of the bottle.

3 Cover the outside of the plastic bottle and the cardboard base with a layer of pulp.

Note The pulp may dry on your fingers as you work. Keep a bowl of water next to you so that you can wet your fingers occasionally to stop this from happening.

Neaten the rim of the goblet by pressing the pulp onto the plastic edge.

5

While the pulp is still wet, put a blob of multipurpose glue on the back of eight glass beads and press them firmly into the pulp around the goblet. Let it dry for forty-eight hours.

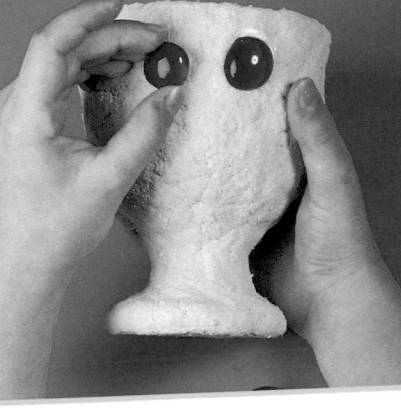

6 Paint the inside and outside of the goblet with metallic acrylic paint.

FURTHER IDEAS

Decorate your goblet using buttons or small pebbles insteud of glass beads.

Indian Frame

The shape of this Indian frame was inspired by the domed roof of the Taj Mahal, a beautiful tomb in India which was built by a **Mogul** Emperor for his wife. The decoration for the frame is based on Indian **saris**—women's clothes that are made of brightly colored cloth and metallic threads. I have used candy wrappers and metallic paint in this project to transform a plain piece of cardboard into a frame to treasure.

! Double **corrugated** cardboard needs to be cut with a craft knife. Ask an adult to do this for you—craft knives are very sharp.

1 Photocopy and enlarge the pattern on page 31. Then cut it out and place it on a piece of double corrugated cardboard. Trace around the pattern with a pencil and cut out the cardboard frame.

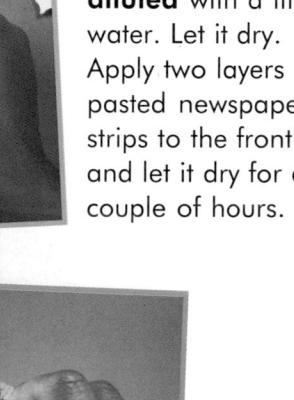

2 Paste both sides of the cardboard frame with multipurpose glue **diluted** with a little water. Let it dry. Apply two layers of pasted newspaper strips to the front and let it dry for a couple of hours.

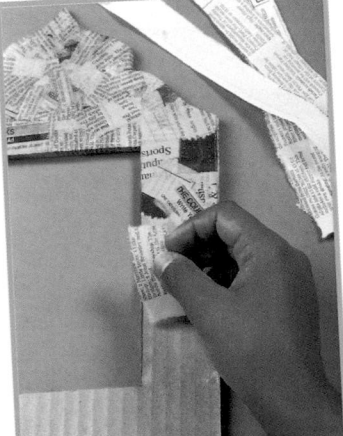

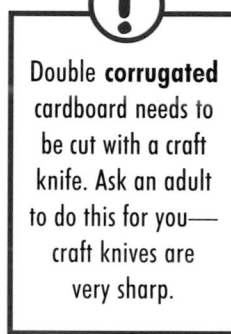

3 Tear foil candy wrappers into irregular shapes. Paste the back of each piece with multipurpose glue and press them onto the cardboard frame. Cover the front and the edges. Overlap the foil pieces onto the back. Let it dry.

4 Pour a little metallic acrylic paint onto a palette. Dip a piece of sponge into the paint and dab it on the outer and inner edges of the frame. Let it dry.

Paint the back of the frame in a color of your choice. Let the paint dry. Cut out a piece of posterboard, slightly bigger than the opening in the frame. Cut a wide "v" shape across the top of the posterboard. Tape the posterboard over the opening, leaving the top untaped. This will create a pocket for your picture or photograph.

FURTHER IDEAS

Create a different effect by decorating your frame with torn pieces of colored tissue paper.

6 Tape a loop of string to the back of the frame for hanging. Insert your picture or photograph.

Carnival Headdress

Some countries in **Latin America** and the **West Indies** have a celebration called Carnival. People wear colorful costumes. This feathered headdress is based on one that might be worn at Carnival.

YOU WILL NEED

Large and small feathers
Colored beads • String
Single corrugated cardboard
Paper pulp • Newspaper • Balloon
Small bowl • **Gesso**
Colored acrylic paint • **Palette**
Paintbrush • Sponge • Scissors
Pencil • Masking tape

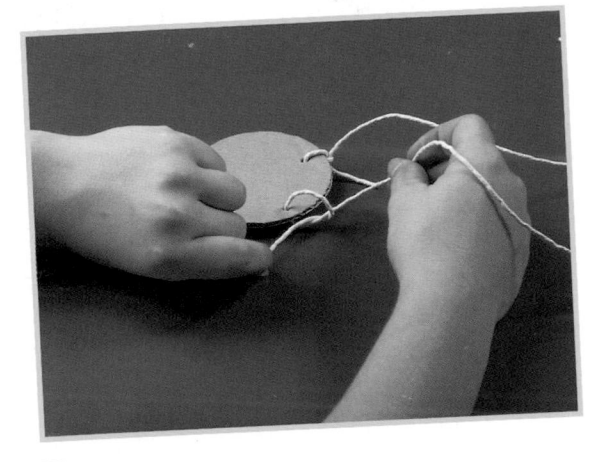

1 Copy and cut out the headdress shape on page 31 from single **corrugated** cardboard. Pierce two holes in each disk shape with the end of a paintbrush. Thread a length of string through each hole and tie to secure.

2 Cover one side of the cardboard with pulp. Leave the corrugations along the top of the cardboard shape uncovered. Later you will stick feathers into these. Add a little more pulp over the circular disk shapes. Roll out a sausage of pulp and press this along the headdress to create a raised zig-zag decoration.

3 Blow up a balloon to approximately the same size as your head. Use masking tape to attach the balloon to a small bowl. Tie the headdress around the balloon and let it dry for forty-eight hours.

4 Prime the headdress with gesso. When dry, decorate with zig-zags and dots of brightly colored acrylic paint.

FURTHER IDEAS
Paint the headband with earthy colors and use natural feathers for a different effect.

5 Sponge the lengths of string with colored paint. When dry, thread the strings at the bottom of the disk shapes with colored beads. Leave the strings at the side unbeaded, so you can tie the headdress around your head.

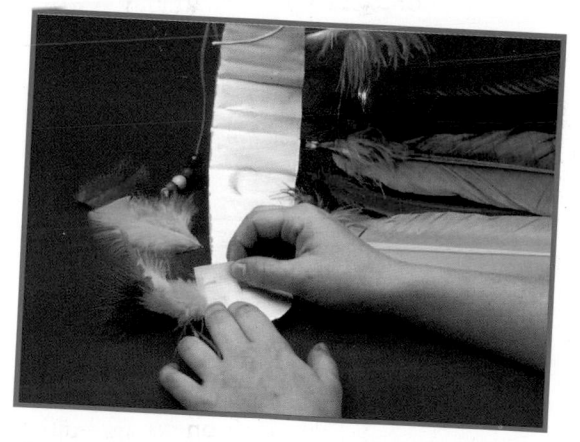

6 Push large colored feathers into the holes along the top of the corrugated card. Then tape two small feathers so they hang down each side.

17

Mexican Bowl

The inspiration for this bright little bowl comes from Mexico. In fact, the art of pot-making originated from the Mexican area because there was a lot of clay in the soil. Traditional Mexican designs use bright colors and geometric designs. In this project, paper pulp is used to make a textured bowl. You can use any bowl as a mold for this project—ceramic, plastic, or glass. It does not matter what size it is. Remember that the finished papier mâché bowl is intended to be **decorative**—you cannot eat out of it!

YOU WILL NEED

Selection of colored beads
8 pieces of leather thong
about 3 inches (20 cm) long
Bowl • Plastic wrap • Paper pulp
Newspaper • **Gesso**
Colored acrylic paint
Paintbrush • **Palette**
Cooling rack

1

Line the inside of a bowl with plastic wrap. Press paper pulp into the bowl with your fingers. When it is about ½ inch (1 cm) thick, smooth the surface with your fingers.

2 Use the end of a paintbrush to make eight holes around the bowl. Try to make the spaces between the holes roughly equal. Let it dry for three hours.

3 Carefully lift the pulp shell out of the bowl using the plastic wrap. Place on a cooling rack and let it dry for at least twenty-four hours.

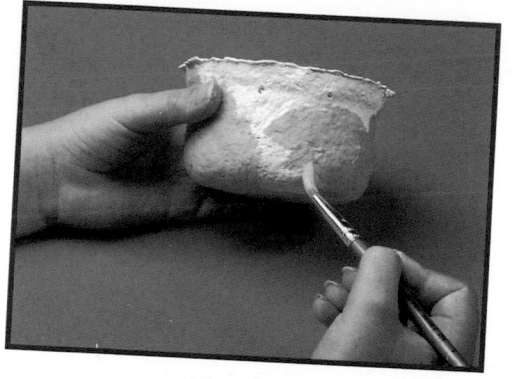

 Prime the bowl with two coats of gesso. Let it dry. Paint the outside of the bowl with colored acrylic paint. Let to dry.

 Paint the inside of the bowl a different color. Let it dry.

6 Tie a knot in a length of leather thong and attach three beads. Thread it through one of the holes in the bowl. Tie a knot on the inside and cut off the end of the thong. Repeat around the bowl.

FURTHER IDEAS
Use brightly colored yarn to decorate your bowl.

Gothic Mirror

Gothic architecture sparked off the idea for this mirror. Some old churches have pointed arches and carved stonework. The mirror in this project is created using a mirror tile on a cardboard base. I have covered the cardboard with paper pulp to create a stone brickwork effect.

YOU WILL NEED
Mirror tile • Paper pulp
Double corrugated cardboard
Newspaper • Masking tape
Multipurpose glue • Paste brush
Natural-colored acrylic paint
Wallpaper paste • Paintbrush
Palette • Ruler • Soft cloth
Cooling rack

1 Cut out the frame shape shown on page 30 from double **corrugated** cardboard. Coat both sides with **diluted** multipurpose glue and allow to dry on a cooling rack.

2 Apply two layers of pasted newspaper strips to the front and back of the frame. Let it dry for four hours.

3 Apply multipurpose glue to the back of the mirror and then press it into place on the front of the frame.

4 Press paper pulp onto the front and edges of the cardboard frame. Smooth the pulp with your fingers as you work.

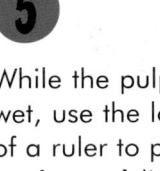
5

While the pulp is still wet, use the long edge of a ruler to press **horizontal** lines into the pulp. Use the short edge of the ruler to create **vertical** lines. This will give the effect of stone brickwork. Let it dry for forty-eight hours.

6 Paint the frame with natural colored paint and polish the mirror with a soft cloth.

Note If the frame starts to warp while the paper pulp is drying, placing something heavy on the mirror tile will help flatten the frame.

FURTHER IDEAS
Make the mirror frame **Norman** rather than Gothic by cutting out a rounded arch.

Aztec Necklace

Aztec craftsmen made beautiful jewelery. They considered **jade** to be their most precious stone, but they also used **onyx**, rock crystal, and **turquoise**. The necklace in this project is made out of pulp that has been decorated with string, foil, and metallic paint.

YOU WILL NEED
Foil • String
Paper pulp • Newspaper
Plastic wrap • Posterboard
Colored and metallic acrylic paint
Gesso • Paintbrush
Sponge • Multipurpose glue
Paste brush • Masking tape
Cooling rack

1 Tape a piece of plastic wrap over a piece of posterboard so that it is stretched tight.

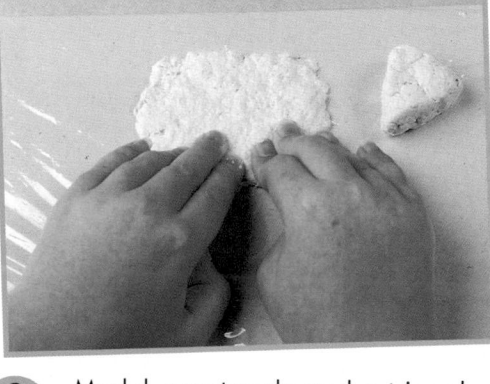

2 Model a rectangle and a triangle of pulp. Press each shape onto the plastic wrap, flattening the shapes with your fingers.

3 Press string into each pulp shape to create swirling patterns.

4 Use the end of a paintbrush to make three holes in the rectangular shape—one in each of the two top corners and one in the middle of the bottom. Make one hole at the top of the triangle. Let them dry for an hour. Carefully remove the shapes from the plastic wrap and let them dry for another twelve hours.

While the pulp is still wet, use the long edge of a ruler to press **horizontal** lines into the pulp. Use the short edge of the ruler to create **vertical** lines. This will give the effect of stone brickwork. Let it dry for forty-eight hours.

6 Paint the frame with natural colored paint and polish the mirror with a soft cloth.

Note If the frame starts to warp while the paper pulp is drying, placing something heavy on the mirror tile will help flatten the frame.

FURTHER IDEAS
Make the mirror frame **Norman** rather than Gothic by cutting out a rounded arch.

Egyptian Cat

The Ancient Egyptians worshipped the cat goddess Bastet and made bronze cat figures dedicated to her. Bastet represented the power of the sun to ripen crops. This project uses a plastic bottle and a **polystyrene** ball as a base for re-creating Bastet. Pulp is used to model her features, and once painted, she is sponged with metallic paint to make her look like a real goddess.

1 Remove the bottle cap and place the polystyrene ball on top of the bottle. Tape the ball into place with long strips of masking tape. Press the tape flat on the bottle to create a smooth finish.

2 Cover the polystyrene ball with a layer of paper pulp. Build up the nose, then model two triangles of pulp to create the ears. Smooth the pulp with your fingers as you work.

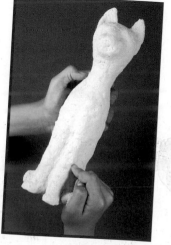

3 Work down the bottle, covering it with pulp. Build up the front legs and feet, then the hind legs and feet using pulp. Neaten the base of the bottle and let it dry for two days.

4 Paint the cat with colored acrylic paint. Let it dry. Paint the eyes and nose in a darker color.

6 Pour a little metallic paint onto a palette. Lightly sponge the cat all over.

5 Paint on the collar with colored and metallic paint and let it dry. Glue on a strip of ribbon around the top of the collar.

FURTHER IDEAS
Look for a picture of the Egyptian god, Anubis, who is represented as a jackal. Try creating a model of its head.

Aztec Necklace

Aztec craftsmen made beautiful jewelery. They considered **jade** to be their most precious stone, but they also used **onyx**, rock crystal, and **turquoise**. The necklace in this project is made out of pulp that has been decorated with string, foil, and metallic paint.

1 Tape a piece of plastic wrap over a piece of posterboard so that it is stretched tight.

2 Model a rectangle and a triangle of pulp. Press each shape onto the plastic wrap, flattening the shapes with your fingers.

3 Press string into each pulp shape to create swirling patterns.

4 Use the end of a paintbrush to make three holes in the rectangular shape—one in each of the two top corners and one in the middle of the bottom. Make one hole at the top of the triangle. Let them dry for an hour. Carefully remove the shapes from the plastic wrap and let them dry for another twelve hours.

Sponge a length of string with metallic paint. Cut off a short piece and use it to link the rectangle and triangle together by threading one end in the hole at the bottom of the rectangular shape, the other end in the hole in the triangular shape, and tying the ends together. Tie two longer pieces of string to the rectangle so that you can hang the necklace around your neck.

5 Prime both pieces with gesso. Let them dry, then paint with acrylic paint in colors of your choice. Let them dry, then lightly sponge both pieces with metallic paint. Roll two small balls of foil and glue one onto each piece.

FURTHER IDEAS

Model round pieces of pulp and attach earring clips to the back to make earrings. Thread round shapes with string to create a bracelet.

Roman Box

Roman city houses were often plain on the outside, but on the inside they were painted with scenes from **mythology** or the countryside. Romans covered their floors with mosaics—pictures and patterns made up from small pieces of stone. This project shows you how to make a simple mosaic box using cardboard, paint, and a potato stamp. I have varnished the finished piece with diluted multipurpose glue to make it look shiny.

YOU WILL NEED
Potato
Single corrugated cardboard
Newspaper • Wallpaper paste
Vegetable knife • Chopping board
Gesso • Colored acrylic paint
Paintbrush • **Palette**
Masking tape • Multipurpose glue
Paste brush
Scissors

1 Cut out four 4¾ inches (12 cm) and two 5½ inches (14 cm) squares from single **corrugated** cardboard. Now cut out one 4¼ inches (11 cm) and one 1½ inches (4 cm) square. Tape the four 4¾ inches (12 cm) squares together with masking tape to form the sides of the box. Tape one 5½ inches (14 cm) square to an open end of the box to create a base.

2 To make a lid, glue the 4¼ inches (11 cm) square to the center of the remaining 5½ inches (14 cm) square. Let the glue dry. Turn over and pierce through the center of the larger square with the end of a paintbrush. Apply a blob of glue to the hole and push a corner of the 1½ inches (4 cm) square into the hole. Secure with small pieces of masking tape.

3 Coat the box and lid with **diluted** multipurpose glue. Let the glue dry. Then apply two layers of pasted newspaper strips to the box. Let it dry for four hours. Prime the box with two coats of gesso. Let it dry.

 Cut a ½ inch (1 cm) wide french fry shape from a potato. Dab it into acrylic paint and use it to stamp the sides of the box.

> ! It is best to cut the potato on a chopping board. Get an adult to help you do this— vegetable knives are very sharp.

5 Stamp three rows of squares around the lid and paint the handle.

6 Paint the rim of the base and the inside of the box. Let it dry. Then apply a coat of diluted multipurpose glue to varnish the outside of the box and the lid.

FURTHER IDEAS
Cut triangular and rectangular shaped potato shapes and use them to stamp a different design on your box.

African Pencil Pot

The inspiration for this project comes from African drums. I have used cardboard tubing to re-create the drum shapes and have decorated the pencil pot with colors typical of traditional African art. It is best to use different sizes of cardboard tubing. You can make a simple pencil pot using just a few tubes, or you can use lots to create a more complicated one.

1 Cut five different lengths of cardboard tubing. Tape the tubes together, making sure that the bases are **level**. Place the tubes on a piece of posterboard and draw around the bases. Cut around this shape and attach it to the bottom of the tubes with masking tape.

2 Apply two layers of pasted newspaper strips over the pencil pot and let it dry for four hours.

3 Prime the pencil pot with gesso and let it dry. Apply a coat of colored acrylic paint. When it is dry, paint colored lines down each tube and a zig zag border around the base. Let the paint dry.

28

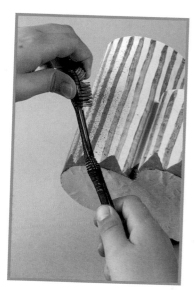

5 Paint a dark border around the base of the pencil pot and add small triangles within the larger colored ones.

6 Paint a dark band around the top of each tube and allow them to dry. Finally, use the same color to paint the inside of the tubes.

4 Dip a toothbrush into **diluted** acrylic paint. Then hold it over the pencil pot and pull back the bristles with your finger. As the bristles slip away from your finger, they will spatter drops of paint on the pencil pot. Wash your hands immediately afterwards.

FURTHER IDEAS
Create a completely different look by decorating with spots and stars instead of stripes and triangles.

Patterns

You can photocopy the patterns on these pages and transfer the designs to cardboard as shown on page 8. Use them the size that they appear here, or make them larger or smaller on a photocopier if you wish.

Get an adult to help you photocopy the patterns.

This pattern is for the Gothic Mirror featured on pages 20–21.

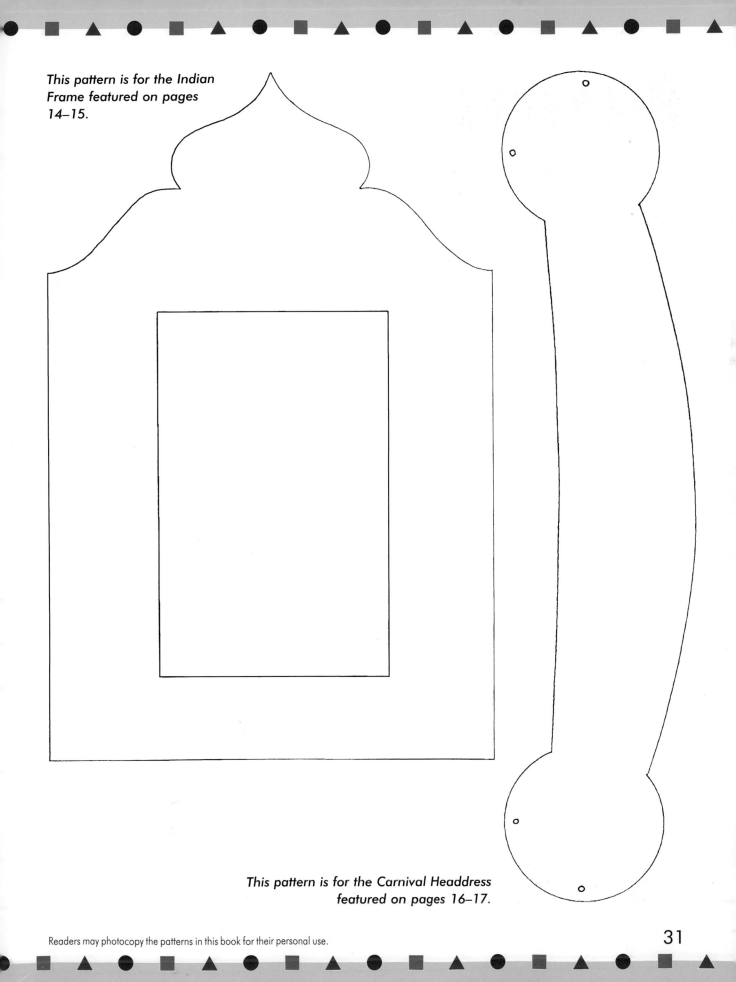

*This pattern is for the Indian
Frame featured on pages
14–15.*

*This pattern is for the Carnival Headdress
featured on pages 16–17.*

Glossary

Aztec people who lived in the 15th and early 16th centuries in what is now central and southern Mexico

Celtic people originally from what is now England; the language of the Celtic people still spoken in areas of Ireland, Scotland, Wales, and Brittany

Corrugated having a layer of ridges or grooves, often between two flat surfaces

Decorative something made purely for the way it looks

Dilute to thin or to make weaker by adding water to a liquid substance

Gesso thick, white paint sold in art supply stores

Goblet glass or cup that has a base and stem

Gothic architecture style of European buildings that lasted roughly from the 13th through the 14th centuries and that is known for pointed arches

Horizontal level with the ground

Jade decorative, green stone that is often used in making jewelry and carvings

Level flat or even; balanced so no side is higher or lower than another

Mogul people who conquered and ruled India from 1526 to 1857

Mythology stories, traditions, or beliefs of a culture, or a particular group of people

Norman architecture style of European buildings that lasted roughly from the 11th through the 12th centuries and that is known for rounded arches

Onyx black stone that is frequently used in making jewelry

Palette thin wooden board or plastic dish used to hold and mix different colors of paint

Polystyrene stiff, plastic foam often used for cups for hot liquids such as coffee and hot chocolate

Sari piece of clothing often worn by Hindu women that is made of a long piece of cotton or silk that wraps around the body and drapes over one shoulder

Turquoise greenish-blue stone found frequently in the southwestern United States and often used in jewelry

Vertical upright, straight up and down

Warp to become bent or twisted out of shape

More Books to Read

Gibson, Ray. *Papier Mâché*. Tulsa, Okla.: EDC Publishing, Inc., 1995.

Papier Mâché. New York: DK Publishing, 1998.

Schwarz, Renee F. *Papier Mâché*. Buffalo, N.Y.: Kids Can Press, 2000.

Index